GOOD QUESTIONS ON

HEAVEN

&

HELL

{ A SIX-SESSION BIBLE STUDY }

Featuring Christianity Today Authors

Standard ®
P U B L I S H I N G

Cincinnati, Ohio

Published by Standard Publishing, Cincinnati, Ohio
www.standardpub.com

Also available: *Good Questions on Belief & Doubt* (ISBN 978-0-7847-2568-9); *Good Questions on Right & Wrong* (ISBN 978-0-7847-2567-2).

Printed in the United States of America

Project editor: Kelli B. Trujillo
Development editor: Laura Derico
Cover design: Faceout®Studio
Interior design: Dina Sorn at Ahaa! Design
Contributing study writers: Christopher Blumhofer, Joy-Elizabeth Lawrence, Michael Mack, Jason & Alison Tarka, David & Kelli Trujillo, Kyle White

The "Good Questions" questions and articles that appear at the beginning of each chapter of *Good Questions on Heaven & Hell* are licensed from and copyright of Christianity Today International. *Christianity Today* magazine and its associated logos are trademarks of Christianity Today International, 465 Gundersen Drive, Carol Stream, Illinois 60188 (ChristianityToday.com).

ISBN 978-0-7847-2566-5

17 16 15 14 13 12 11   1 2 3 4 5 6 7 8 9

• CONTENTS •

• INTRODUCTION •
WHAT'S IN THIS BOOK?

Everyone has questions. Some are easy: What can I wear today? Should I eat Fruity O's or Sugar Circles? Where did I put my keys? Some are heavy: What should I do with my life? Is this wrong or right? Where is God when I need him?

It's true that some people ask questions to distract, deceive, delay, or to stir up dissension. But good questions do something different. Good questions make us wonder, search, stretch, and grow.

With the Good Question Bible Studies series, we hope to help you cultivate an environment in which honest questions are welcomed, and the answers are sought together both through the consultation of respected research and through the experience of respectful—though no doubt often lively—conversation.

Each session begins with a question—a good question—which has been selected from some of those posed by readers and published in a feature section of *Christianity Today*. That question is followed by an article that was written in response by a well-known Christian author, experienced leader, and/or seasoned scholar.

But this is not where the study ends. **Launch** gives you a chance to open up the conversation with your group and build relationships through optional exercises. **Engage** allows the discussion to grow, building on the study of relevant Scripture passages. **Respond** and **React** ask you to reflect on the ideas you've talked about and think about what actions you might take. And finally, **Stretch** challenges each member to take the discussion beyond the group and into their relationships with others.

Throughout the studies **Delve Deeper** features provide an opportunity for more thought, while **For Further Study** lists point you in the direction of useful resources.

As every member uses these books, you will find that Good Question Bible Studies do not provide easy answers. But you will be met with an irresistible challenge: to wrestle with the issues and grow sharper, stronger, and closer to each other—and to God—along the way.

If your group enjoys these studies, don't miss the other titles in this series: *Good Questions on Belief & Doubt* (ISBN 978-0-7847-2568-9) and *Good Questions on Right & Wrong* (ISBN 978-0-7847-2567-2).

WHAT HAPPENS NEXT?
{ THE BIBLE IS OUR GUIDE IN MATTERS OF LIFE AND DEATH }

Before you meet with your small group, read this good question. Then read the response article written by J. I. Packer.

GQ 1 Hebrews 9:27 says, "[M]an is destined to die once, and after that to face judgment." **Does Scripture say why God ends the choice for or against Jesus as Savior at physical death?** If God were to extend the opportunity for even thirty seconds after physical death, what a difference that might make!

When the writer of Hebrews speaks of dying "once," he uses a word that means not once merely as distinct from two or more times, but "once and for all." The adverb (hapax in Greek) points to the decisiveness of the event it qualifies; by happening once, the event changes things permanently so that the possibility of it happening again is removed. That is what the word means when it is applied in verses 26 and 28 to Jesus' atoning sacrifice of himself on the cross, and in verse 27 it means the same when applied to the event of our own heart-stop and brain-stop and the separating of the self from the corpse.

The unrepeatable reality of physical death leads directly to reaping what we sowed in this world. So Jesus taught in his tale of the callous rich man and Lazarus the beggar (Luke 16:19-31), and when he spoke of dying in one's sins as something supremely dreadful (John 8:21-23). So Paul taught when he affirmed that, on judgment day, all received a destiny corresponding to their works; that is, to the decisive direction of their lives (Romans 2:5-16; Galatians 6:7, 8; 2 Corinthians 5:10). The New Testament is solid in viewing death and judgment this way.

> What sort of event is a "choice for or against Jesus as Savior"? The phrase might suggest it is like choosing the preferred dish from a menu.

Modern theologians are not all solid here. Some of them expect that some who did not embrace Christ in this life may yet do so savingly in the life to come. Some who expect this are evangelicals who think that the God of grace owes everyone a clear presentation of the gospel in terms they understand. Others who expect an exercise of postmortem faith are universalists, for whom it is axiomatic that all humans will finally enjoy God in heaven, and therefore that God must and will continue to exert loving pressure till all have been drawn to Christ. So John Hick posits as many postmortem lives for each non-Christian as is necessary to this end, and Nels Ferré describes hell as having "a school and a door" in it: when those in hell come to their senses about Christ they may leave, so that the place ends up empty. But this is nonscriptural speculation and reflects an inadequate grasp of what turning to Christ involves.

What sort of event is a "choice for or against Jesus as Savior"? The phrase might suggest it is like choosing the preferred dish from a menu—a choice where you opt for what strikes you as the best of the bunch, knowing that if your first choice is not available, a second is always possible. But coming savingly to Christ is not like that. When it occurs, there is a sense of inevitability about it, springing from three sources: the pressure of gospel truth that feels too certain to be denied, plus the sense of God's presence forcing one to face the reality of Jesus Christ, plus the realization that without him, one is lost, currently ruining oneself and desperately needing to be changed. This sense is generated by God's prevenient grace—his action of making the first move. There is no commitment to Christ (no "choice for Jesus," if one prefers to say it that way) apart from this convicting divine action. The nature and necessity of regeneration (for that is what this is) was never a matter of dispute between Puritan Calvinists and Wesleyan Arminians.

The act of the heart in choosing Jesus Christ is not always performed in a single moment, nor is it always performed calmly and clear-headedly. At surface level there are often crosscurrents of reluctance. C. S. Lewis, dissecting his own conversion story (Surprised by Joy), wrote of "the steady, unrelenting approach of him whom I so earnestly desired not to meet," and scoffed at the idea that anyone really seeks the real God and the real, living Christ, with their dominating, dictatorial demands for discipleship. ("You might as well speak of the mouse's search for the cat.") But in every real conversion, prevenient grace (meaning, as is now clear, the Holy Spirit) ensures a real change of heart through the Calvary love of Christ becoming irresistible.

> How a just-dead person's perceptions differ from what they were before is more than we have been told.

How a just-dead person's perceptions differ from what they were before is more than we have been told. But Scripture says nothing of prevenient grace triggering postmortem conversions, and that being so, we should conclude that the unbeliever's lack of desire for Christ and the Father and heaven *remains unchanged. So for God to extend the offer of salvation beyond the moment of death, even for thirty seconds, would be pointless. Nothing would come of it.*

J. I. Packer is Board of Governors' Professor of Theology at Regent College and a member of the editorial council for Christianity Today. *"Can the Dead Be Converted?" was first published in the January 1999 issue of* Christianity Today.

LAUNCH

OPTIONAL EXERCISE

Your group may want to begin your meeting with this activity. Someone will need to print off or photocopy in advance the **lyrics** to a few well-known hymns, spirituals, and/or popular praise songs (depending on what your audience is likely to be familiar with) and distribute these lyrics to everyone in your group. (Use an Internet search or borrow some good hymnbooks.)

Sing together at least one song that places its hope in the life to come, for example, "I'll Fly Away," "Amazing Grace," or "I'm Just a Poor Wayfaring Stranger." (Do your best to pick songs that have an easy-to-sing melody. If someone in your group is a singer or a musician, ask that person to lead you.)

After singing, reflect on the lyrics together. Discuss how you see life, death, Heaven, and Hell portrayed in the songs. Compare and contrast the ideas in the lyrics with how our current culture thinks about life, death, and the afterlife.

American theologian Stanley Hauerwas sometimes poses this question to his audiences: "How do you want to die?"[1]

Most modern people answer that question by saying things like "quickly" or "in my sleep." But that is very much a twenty-first-century way of answering the question. At one point in history, Hauerwas points out, dying suddenly was the worst of all possible deaths—it meant that a person might face God before making peace with his or her neighbors, and before making peace with God. Today, we think about death almost entirely in terms of a single moment. In the past, however, thinking about death was conditioned by what happened after death. If a person wished to die well, he or she would prepare by living well.

Jesus (in Matthew 25), Paul (in 2 Corinthians 5:9, 10), and the writer of Hebrews (in Hebrews 9:27) all connect life, death, and the judgment we will receive from God. As they describe it, for some people judgment will result in rewards; for others, criticism and condemnation.

1   From a biblical perspective, what would be your answer to the question "How do you want to die?"

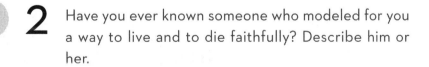

2   Have you ever known someone who modeled for you a way to live and to die faithfully? Describe him or her.

Keeping in mind the Bible's conviction that life, death, and judgment are all deeply connected, let's consider three significant biblical perspectives on what happens when we die.

ENGAGE

JESUS CHRIST IS THE SAVIOR AND THE JUDGE OF THE WORLD

In the opening chapters of Romans, Paul lays out his understanding of grace and guilt, forgiveness and judgment. The Gentiles, who *did not* receive the laws and covenants of the Old Testament, will be judged by Jesus, writes Paul (in Romans 2:12-16). The Jews, who *did* receive the laws and covenants of the Old Testament, will be judged by Jesus as well (Romans 3:9-26). Everything centers on Jesus Christ.

Read **Romans 8:31-39**. Here Paul draws on Jesus' role as the judge of the world in order to comfort the church in Rome.

1 Why do you think Paul considers it comforting that our Savior is also our judge?

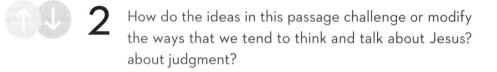

2 How do the ideas in this passage challenge or modify the ways that we tend to think and talk about Jesus? about judgment?

In his own testimony about salvation and judgment in John 3, Jesus emphasizes that salvation comes through faith in himself. But he goes on to talk about the relationship between how we live and what we believe. Read **John 3:14-21** and take a close look at what Jesus says.

 3 According to this passage, what's the relationship between faith, salvation, and the ways that we live? How does this compare or contrast with how we normally tend to think about faith, salvation, and a person's lifestyle?

THE COMING JUDGMENT SHOULD CHANGE HOW WE LIVE

In his *Christianity Today* article, J. I. Packer writes that "on judgment day, all [receive] a destiny corresponding to their works." Paul the apostle develops the same idea about the eternal standing of our works—our actions, words, and choices—when he instructs the Corinthians about the coming resurrection and judgment. He concludes his teaching in 1 Corinthians 15 with this encouragement: "Therefore, my dear brothers, stand firm. Let nothing move you. Always give yourselves fully to the work of the Lord, because you know that your labor in the Lord is not in vain" (v. 58).

DELVE DEEPER

If you'd like, explore this question as a group or on your own:

1 Corinthians 3 records Paul's teachings about how our works will be judged on the last day. Paul is specifically writing about leaders of the church and how their teachings and leadership build up the community, but his words give us a glimpse of how judgment comes even for Christians. Read 1 Corinthians 3:10-17.

How do we reconcile Paul's words about salvation coming through faith (Ephesians 2:8, 9) with teachings like this one, about a day on which even believers are judged for their faithfulness (or lack of faithfulness)?

It seems strange to think that the day of judgment could actually be a source of support for how we live today, but that is exactly what Paul insists: because we know what tomorrow holds, we can find strength to live for today. He makes a similar point in 2 Corinthians 5:10: "For we must all appear before the judgment seat of Christ, that each one may receive what is due him for the things done while in the body, whether good or bad." This means that the ways in which we live and the choices we make have profound importance.

4 Have you ever had to make a decision that seemed painful in the here-and-now, but you knew had significance in light of eternity? What happened?

5 Make Paul's teaching personal: What's one thing in your life that you would like to do differently or one area of your life to which you'd like to give greater attention, knowing that the ways we live are not "in vain," but are critically important for how we will be judged by God?

J. I. Packer also explains in his article that **Hebrews 9:27** ("Just as man is destined to die once, and after that to face judgment") emphasizes the finality of death. He writes: "The unrepeatable reality of physical death leads directly to reaping what we sowed in this world."

The idea of reaping what we sow has kept many Christians from being passive or being reckless in how they live. It has also motivated many practical responses—joyous worship, fervent intercession, humble service, and also energetic evangelism. All of these responses are appropriate.

6 What would you say if another Christian told you that the way a person lives does not matter as long as he has prayed and asked Christ into his heart? Explain.

GOD IS THE ONE WHO HOLDS THE POWER OF JUDGMENT

Reflecting on Scripture's teaching about Heaven and Hell, Bible scholar N. T. Wright says in his book *Surprised by Hope* that "God is utterly committed to set the world right in the end . . . And that setting right must necessarily involve the elimination of all that distorts God's good and lovely creation and in particular of all that defaces his image-bearing human creatures."[2] Wright's idea of "setting the world right" challenges us to think about Heaven and Hell not only in terms of punishment and rewards, but also in broader terms of how God's judgment will fulfill God's redemptive work.

7 Read one of the most vivid New Testament descriptions of judgment, **Matthew 25:31-46.** How does this portrayal of divine judgment inform your understanding of God's redemptive work on earth and the part he intends us to play?

Many people today are especially allergic to the idea of judgment and Hell because they believe that it would be unfair for God to judge people who never had the opportunity to come to faith. Scripture teaches, however, that Jesus Christ is the judge of all people, and that he is a *just* judge.

8 Read **Romans 2:1-16**. What does this passage teach us, both about how others will be judged and how we are to think about the judgment of others? Summarize it in your own words.

It's easy to forget that Jesus warned his hearers about judgment and Hell more than any person in the Bible. Hell is real and it is the wrath that all people deserve. Jesus saved us from that wrath on the cross. While Jesus warns us of Hell, he also speaks clearly about God's desire to save us: "For God did not send his Son into the world to condemn the world, but to save the world through him" (John 3:17). Judgment is understood as the shadow side of the amazing love that God offers to us through Jesus.

9 How would you explain to a friend the idea that Jesus came not simply to judge the world, but to save it?

10 Why is it important that we keep a proper perspective on Heaven, Hell, and judgment? What is at risk if we let one of those three block out the reality of the others?

RESPOND

Imagine that a friend came to you and confessed that he or she is scared to face death because no one knows what happens when we die. In light of your group discussion, what would you say to your friend about what Christians believe about life, death, and judgment?

REACT

Write your reactions: During this study, how has God challenged the way that you think about life, death, and the judgment that all people will face? What is one practical thing that you would like to do

FOR FURTHER STUDY
BOOKS

- *The Art of Dying: Living Faithfully into the Life to Come* by Rob Moll (InterVarsity)
- *Exploring & Proclaiming the Apostles' Creed* by Roger Van Harn, ed. (Eerdmans)
- *Heaven* by Randy Alcorn (Tyndale)
- *Knowing God* by J. I. Packer (InterVarsity)
- *Letters from the Land of Cancer* by Walter Wangerin Jr. (Zondervan)
- *Living Well and Dying Faithfully* by John Swinton and Richard Payne, eds. (Eerdmans)
- *Surprised by Hope: Rethinking Heaven, the Resurrection, and the Mission of the Church* by N. T. Wright (HarperOne)

ONLINE ARTICLES

- "Death & Dying" articles and reflections available from *Christianity Today* (www.christianitytoday.com/ct/special/deathanddying.html)
- "The Echo and Insufficiency of Hell" by John Piper (in two parts) available from Desiring God (www.desiringgod.org)

differently as you respond to the teachings of God's Word on these topics?

End your time praying together as a group. Consider using an A.C.T.S. prayer (Adoration, Confession, Thanksgiving, Supplication) or some other format that allows your prayer to focus both on God's grace and on how we should respond to that grace.

STRETCH

Set aside time on your own after your small group meeting for conversation with a non-Christian friend or family member.

Meet with your friend and share what you learned in this study. In particular, share what it would mean for you to live well in light of what Scripture teaches about life after death. Then pose some of these questions to your friend:

- What does living well mean to you?
- Who in your life has shown you what it means to live well?
- What would it mean for you to die well?

Talking about these topics will quickly cut to the heart of what you and your friend believe about ultimate issues. View your conversation as a chance to deepen your relationship and build a bridge toward later sharing the hope that you have in God. But for now, just listen empathetically and ask questions that will help you understand your friend. Before you're finished, invite your friend to share what he or she sees in your life. Ask: When you look at the way I live, can you tell what my hope is in?

After you've met—or perhaps as you wrap up your time together— spend some time praying that God would strengthen you in faith, hope, and love, so that you can learn what it means to live well and to die well.

Study written by Christopher Blumhofer. His writings have appeared in *Leadership* journal, *Relevant,* and BuildingChurchLeaders.com.

CAN UNFAILING LOVE AND ETERNAL TORTURE GO TOGETHER?
{ MAKING SENSE OF HELLFIRE, BRIMSTONE, AND GNASHING OF TEETH }

PREPARE

Before you meet with your small group, read this good question. Then read the response article written by R. Todd Mangum.

GQ 2 **Is Hell nothing more than eternal torture of the unsaved?**
Why would God engage in punishment that seems so cruel?

God would not be party to anything as sordid as torture; Christians can agree on that. However, theologians are divided about how eternal judgment is not tantamount to such.

Two competing answers are proposed: 1) Yes, hell involves eternal pain inflicted on the unsaved, but this should not be regarded as gratuitous, unjust, or cruel; and 2) the final judgment will not involve eternal, conscious torment as has been traditionally assumed, and this misreading of biblical teaching needs modification. Both sides raise legitimate concerns worth careful consideration.

The first position is the view of most Christians. It argues that people commonly underestimate the appropriate punishment for defying an infinitely holy God. When human rebellion wrecked God's original good design, God undertook, at great cost, to restore humans to a loving relationship with himself. Those who spurn God's love deserve their eternal destiny, justly suffering the pain of God's wrath.

Of course, God alone has the right to execute this type of sentence. And God gets no sadistic enjoyment from pain he inflicts (Ezekiel 18:23, 32). In righteousness and justice, God exacts deadly retribution for wickedness on those not under the blood atonement of Christ.

Other Christians argue that God would never be so seemingly punitive or vicious. They say the Bible's imagery occasionally reflects vindictive presuppositions of ancient cultures, but no one should take this imagery literally. Since rejection of God's love is reprehensible, they say, God will ultimately (and here the answers vary): overcome all evil and all resistance (universalism), destroy all evil (annihilationism), or inflict only as much pain as is necessary to extract repentance, leaving only the incorrigibly evil in everlasting pain (a purgatorial view of hell).

> When human rebellion wrecked God's original good design, God undertook, at great cost, to restore humans to a loving relationship with himself.

As we contemplate the questions raised by hell, it is helpful to remember two strands of complementary biblical teaching. First, just sentences for sin, as described in Scripture, are both proportional and prorated. Divine punishment is meted out in accordance with the severity of a crime and the awareness a person had of God and of sin. To whom much is given, much is required.

The deuteronomic code forbade beating a guilty person be-yond forty lashes, lest the person be "degraded" (Deuteronomy 25:3). In addition, although a person guilty of heinous crimes might be executed, nowhere was infliction of pain over a lengthy period of time commanded or countenanced. That is partly why medieval Christians constructed an elaborate purgatorial scheme, which allowed for varying levels and lengths of suffering, and which posited a host of variables that God might take into account in rendering verdicts (see Luke 12:47, 48). In purgatorial hell, only incorrigibly evil people suffered a limitless duration of pain (see Revelation 14:9-11). This view has never been common among Protestants, but believing in purgatory as the state that purifies and hell as the state of eternal damnation continues to be an official teaching of the Roman Catholic Church.

Second, we must remember that it is never cruel for God to enforce penalties appropriate to crimes committed. Pity toward the guilty is actually suppressed in the Old Testament (Deuteronomy 7:2, 16; 19:21; 25:12). We sometimes assume that this stands in contrast to Christ and his work. It does not. In-deed, God in the Old Testament may have overlooked some wrongs as a concession to the immaturity of his people, but he never forbade them to do something (showing pity to the guilty, in this case) that Jesus later declared to be godly. Jesus came to fulfill the Old Testament, not to overturn it.

The prophets warn that God executes his wrath without pity (Jeremiah 13:14; Ezekiel 5:11-13; 7:4-9; 8:18). Jesus and the New Testament writers confirm that God's future outpouring of wrath will be horrific (Matthew 13:40-42, 48-50; 2 Thessa-lonians 1:5-9). If such biblical descriptions of God's character strike us as harsh, perhaps we need to consider whether our thinking has been compromised by the sentimentalist human-ism of our culture.

Studying the views of theologians throughout history can give us insight into how God's loving reconciliation may be consummated along with his righteous judgment. But in the end, we are simply called to trust—to put our faith in the goodness of God, knowing that he will do what is right and that he will not acquit the unrepentant guilty.

R. Todd Mangum is Professor of Theology and Dean of the Faculty at Biblical Seminary in Hatfield, Pennsylvania. "Three Models of Hell" was first published in the February 2007 issue of Christianity Today.

LAUNCH

OPTIONAL EXERCISE

Your group may want to begin with this activity. Imagine you're a sociologist doing research on Americans' beliefs about the afterlife. Individually, take your best guess at the answers to these questions:

    a. What percentage of Americans believe there is an afterlife? _____

    b. What percentage believe in Heaven? _____

    c. What percentage believe in Hell? _____

    d. What percentage believe they're going to Heaven? _____

    e. What percentage believe they're going to Hell? _____

When you're done, compare your answers with the rest of your group. Then turn to page 34 to review actual data compiled by sociologists.

Talk together about how the real findings compare or contrast with your guesses. Do any of the actual results surprise you? What do *your* non-Christian friends generally believe about Hell?

"A loving God would not send people to Hell."

You've probably heard this before; it's a common attack on Christian belief. From a Christian perspective, right off the bat it seems like an unfair statement. The operative words (*loving*, *send*, and *Hell*) are all used in an overly simplistic way and betray some basic misunderstandings. But this statement isn't just about logic or reason—it points to a real emotional hurdle that many people, even Christians, struggle to overcome.

 1 Empathize for a moment with a skeptic—step into his or her shoes. How would you state the "problem of Hell"? What exactly about the idea of Hell would bother you?

 2 Now, from the perspective of a Christian, what seems especially difficult to accept regarding the idea of Hell? How do your concerns about the doctrine of Hell differ from the hypothetical response of a skeptic?

ENGAGE

THE CONCEPT OF HELL IS NOT IN CONFLICT WITH THE CHARACTER OF GOD

According to philosopher C. Stephen Evans, "the doctrine of hell constitutes the single most difficult version of the problem of evil."[1] The idea that God would allow evil and suffering to exist in

DELVE DEEPER

If you'd like, explore this question as a group or on your own:

Hades is used ten times in the New Testament (see Matthew 11:23; 16:18; Luke 10:15; 16:23; Acts 2:27, 31; Revelation 1:18; 6:8; 20:13, 14); many English translations of Scripture render it as *hell*. Though *Hades* is related to the afterlife, this term is biblically distinct from the *Gehenna* concept of Hell.

The scholarly consensus on *Hades* is that it generally represents the power of death or the temporary place for the dead associated with those who will be eternally cast into Hell. *Hades* is also personified in Scripture, and can be understood as an enemy to God's plan of redemption and life for his people.

Review some of the *Hades* passages listed above. How do these passages complement, clarify, or strengthen your understanding of Hell?

this temporary, earthly life is difficult enough to accept. But when we consider that God's master plan includes eternal suffering for those who reject him, the stakes are raised even higher. At times, we may wish we could simply erase this difficult concept from our theology, but Scripture consistently points to Hell's reality.

The most commonly used New Testament Greek word for Hell is *Gehenna*, literally the Valley of Hinnom, a place located south of Jerusalem. In Matthew 10:28 and Luke 12:5, *Gehenna* is used to demonstrate the authority of Christ as he "has the power to throw you into hell," a place of judgment. The word *Gehenna* is also linked twice to the idea of an "eternal fire" (Matthew 18:8, 9; Mark 9:43-47), emphasizing its permanent nature. In Matthew 5:22-30, there are repeated references to Hell (*Gehenna)* as the destination for unrepentant sinners. And, in Matthew 23:15, 33, Hell is identified as the destination for the hypocritical religious leaders.

Building upon these basic biblical teachings about Hell, read **Matthew 8:10-12, 22:1-14,** and **24:51** aloud. (If you have time, also look at Matthew 13:42-50, 25:30.) Next, read **2 Thessalonians 1:9** and **2 Peter 2:17.**

1 New Testament scholar Craig L. Blomberg notes that Matthew's refrain of "weeping and gnashing of teeth" emphasizes "the agony" of separation from God.[2] In addition to *agony*, brainstorm other words or phrases that describe Hell based on these passages.

Christians can assume either a literal or nonliteral interpretation of the biblical passages describing Hell. A literal view takes the biblical descriptions of Hell (torture, worms, fire, darkness, thirst, and so on) to be the actual physical reality in the next life for those who reject God in this life. In this view, for example, nonbelievers are literally burned by fire for eternity. A nonliteral view understands the descriptions of Hell (fire and so on) to be symbolic, using earthly imagery to communicate the horrifically painful existence of those who are eternally separated from God. This nonliteral understanding of Hell parallels a metaphorical interpretation of the Bible's descriptions of Heaven. For example, a description of Heaven having streets of gold can be understood as a word picture that gives us a glimpse of Heaven's grandeur, rather than an accurate depiction of the construction of Heaven's highways.

2 Of these two basic stances, which best represents the way you understand and interpret Scripture's descriptions of Hell? How so?

The idea of the painful, eternal existence of those in Hell naturally prompts us to consider the character of God. Theologians Gordon Lewis and Bruce Demarest identify at least ten main attributes of God: He is holy, personal, living, active, eternal, loving, almighty, wise, just, and merciful.[3]

3 In your view, which attributes of God are particularly important in the way we understand the doctrine of Hell? What other attributes might you add to this list in light of the doctrine of Hell?

4 Some skeptics claim that the doctrine of Hell compromises our assertions about God's character. How might you begin to answer such a claim?

C. Stephen Evans suggests, "since we know that God is a God of love and mercy as well as justice, we can be confident that he will do what is loving and merciful as well as just. Our confidence in the character of God, then, should outweigh the confidence we have in our theories about hell."[4] Likewise, Mangum concludes his article by saying "we are simply called to trust—to put our faith in the goodness of God, knowing that he will do what is right and that he will not acquit the unrepentant guilty."

5 Scripture repeatedly describes God's wrath. Mangum suggests that our thinking about such descriptions may have "been compromised by the sentimentalist humanism of our culture." What do you think he means by "sentimentalist humanism"? To what extent do you agree or disagree with this assertion?

HELL IS FOR THOSE WHO REJECT GOD AND HIS KINGDOM

Christian theology is one cohesive unit. The doctrine of Hell cannot be adequately understood in isolation; it must be viewed in light of the doctrine of sin. As Scripture clearly asserts, we are all sinners (Romans 3:23) and are deserving of death and separation from God (6:23).

6 How does our culture view "sin"? How do you think this modern-day conception of sin has affected our ability to properly understand the doctrine of Hell?

7 Read Jesus' teachings in **Luke 13:22-30** and **16:19-31**. What do these teachings add to your understanding of the nature of Hell, the character of God, and human responsibility? Be specific.

In Luke 13, Jesus clearly contrasts those who "know" God from those who don't. And in Luke 16, Jesus draws a sharp distinction between poor Lazarus and the rich man. Jesus and other biblical writers regularly use the "rich" to more broadly symbolize those who live for themselves in this life rather than living by God's values and Jesus' teachings about his kingdom. So, in Jesus' parable, we may feel a sense of justice as, it appears, the rich man gets what he deserves.

 8 Do you agree with the sentiment expressed above? Does the idea of Hell ever provide you with a sense of comfort or justice? Explain.

HELL IS BEST UNDERSTOOD IN CONTRAST TO HEAVEN

Jesus creates a clear dichotomy in the Gospels between the wicked and the righteous (Matthew 25:32), the followers and rejecters (Mark 4:1-20), and the insiders and outsiders (Luke 13:25). In Matthew 12:30, Jesus stridently declares, "He who is not with me is against me."

This contrast directly extends to the eternal destinations of the righteous and wicked described in Revelation. People will either be "thrown into the lake of fire" (20:15) or dwell in God's city where the river of life flows "down the middle of the great street" (22:1, 2). Hell is a place void of God's presence, whereas Heaven is *filled* with God's sustaining presence. Hell is a place of no rest or peace, whereas Heaven is distinctly characterized by the rest and peace it offers (Revelation 21:4).

9 How can our understanding of Heaven—what it's like and how we get there—nuance and clarify our understanding of Hell? Explain.

DELVE DEEPER

If you'd like, explore this question as a group or on your own:

From the fall in Genesis onward, we see humanity's disobedience—with the result of death and separation from God. The pervasive contamination of sin touches us all. It is only through accepting Jesus' gift of redemption and surrendering our lives to him that we escape the punishment we deserve and receive the gift of eternal life with God (see Romans 3:21-26).

Some Christian apologists use this line of reasoning in response to skeptics who ask why God would "send" people to Hell. Separation from God in Hell, they say, is simply a continuation of the choice to live in separation from God in this earthly life.

Do you think this is an adequate explanation for what Hell is like and why people go there? Why or why not?

Peering into the doctrine of Hell forces us to look at the whole of Christian theology. The "problems" of Hell are easier to navigate when we hold a complete, composite picture of biblical truth. If we consider the idea of Hell in isolation, it certainly does seem overly harsh. But if we view it in relation to God's holiness, human responsibility, and Heaven, we can see its rightness and necessity.

10 Hypothetically speaking, what harm would be done to Christian theology if the doctrine of Hell were eliminated?

RESPOND

The topic of Hell is one of those controversies that will never go away; it's genuinely perplexing and it will remain a difficulty for spiritual seekers considering Christianity. Yet, not only is the doctrine biblical, it is *defensible*. Based on your discussion, how would your response to a skeptic be amended, changed, or simply strengthened (see Launch)? How can you maintain a sense of sympathy with a skeptic's questions while affirming the truth about Hell?

REACT

Write your reactions: In a study like this one, it's easy to think of how this might apply to your interaction with others. Instead, though, consider how your study of Hell has affected *you* personally. Was the study encouraging or challenging in a way that you did not expect?

Gather back together as a group and pray, praising God by affirming his character. Take turns naming aloud what you believe about who God is and what God is like.

STRETCH

Set aside time on your own after your small group meeting to research the position of those who reject the idea of Hell.

Search for a fair and intelligent critique of the orthodox Christian view of Hell on the Internet (they abound!). Read the article empathetically, considering how you might respond to specific concerns raised by a skeptic. Take notes on the author's best points. Aim to identify which of his or her concerns about Hell are based in reason and which may be more based in emotion.

Then revisit the content of this study, especially the Scriptures that deal directly with the issue; use a concordance to find and read additional Scriptures. Imagine yourself in dialogue with the article; how might you answer the skeptic's contentions? How do you imagine the skeptic might respond to your assertions?

FOR FURTHER STUDY
BOOKS

- *Four Views on Hell* by William Crockett and Stanley N. Grundy, eds. (Zondervan)
- *The Great Divorce* by C. S. Lewis (Harper One)
- *The Problem of Pain* by C. S. Lewis (Harper One)
- *Sense & Nonsense About Heaven & Hell* by Kenneth Boa and Robert M. Bowman Jr. (Zondervan)

ONLINE ARTICLES

- "Brimstone for the Broadminded" by Tim Keller, from *Christianity Today* (christianity today.com/ct/1998/july13/8t8065.html)
- "Hell's Final Enigma" by J. I. Packer, from *Christianity Today* (christianitytoday.com/ct/2002/april22/27.84.html)
- "When Your Loved One Doesn't Come to Christ" by JoHannah Reardon, from Kyria .com (Christianity Today International), available at www.kyria.com/topics/missionallife/outreach/loveddoesnt comechrist.html

This study was written by David and Kelli B. Trujillo. David is a Bible teacher and Kelli is an author and editor (www.kellitrujillo.com). They are columnists for *GROUP* magazine and serve together as adult ministry leaders in their church in Indianapolis.

Answers for Launch Optional Exercise

1. According to the Barna Group, 81 percent of Americans believe in life after death.

2. A recent Gallup poll found that 81 percent of Americans believe in Heaven.

3. According to Gallup, 71 percent of Americans believe in Hell; the Pew Forum on Religion and Public Life, on the other hand, finds that only 59 percent of Americans believe Hell is real.

4. The Barna Group reports that 64 percent of Americans expect to go to Heaven; in a similar Gallup Poll, 77 percent of Americans rated their "chances" of going to Heaven as "good" or "excellent."

5. Less than 1 percent of Americans believe they will go to Hell, according to the Barna Group; Gallup research has found that only 6 percent of Americans think there is a high "chance" they will go to Hell after death.[5]

WILL UNBELIEVERS SIMPLY CEASE TO EXIST?

{ WHAT THE BIBLE REALLY SAYS ABOUT ANNIHILATIONISM }

PREPARE

Before you meet with your small group, read this good question. Then read the response article written by Stanley Grenz.

GQ 3 **What is the teaching that says the unsaved will be annihilated rather than suffer eternally in Hell?** Can this belief be part of evangelical theology?

The traditional teaching of the church—that the lost will suffer unending conscious torment in hell—has repeatedly been challenged by "universalists" since the third century. They believe that in the end, all will be saved. After the Reformation, a third viewpoint, "annihilationism," emerged as a minority position—for example, in the 1660 confession of the General Baptists, and among the Seventh-day Adventists and several other evangelical groups in the nineteenth century. Since 1960, several prominent British evangelicals, as well as Canadian theologian Clark Pinnock, have embraced this view. John Stott has likewise expressed sympathy for annihilationism while choosing to remain "agnostic" on the question.

One key difference between universalists and annihilationists is that annihilationists agree with traditionalists that many will indeed be lost eternally. By this, however, they mean that the unsaved will cease to exist for all eternity. They argue that because eternal torment serves no remedial purpose, the traditional concept of hell paints a portrait of God as a vindictive despot incompatible with the loving Father revealed in Jesus. Further, they claim that the presence of people in hell throughout eternity contradicts the Christian truth that Christ has conquered every evil foe and God will reconcile all things in Christ.

Annihilationists agree with traditionalists that many will indeed be lost eternally.

Some annihilationists who are better described as holding to "conditional immortality" claim the idea of eternal conscious punishment depends on the Greek concept of the immortality of the soul, which they say is wrongly read back into the Bible. The Bible teaches, they argue, that we are dependent on God for life, so only through participation in Christ's resurrection are the saved given immortality.

Annihilationists believe the Bible teaches that the end of the wicked is destruction, not eternal torment. Building from the Old Testament (Psalm 37; Malachi 4), they point to how Jesus declared that the wicked will be cast into the smoldering garbage heap of Gehenna (Matthew 5:30), where they will be burned up (Matthew 3:10-12) and destroyed in both body and soul (Matthew 10:28). Similarly, Paul spoke of the fate of the lost as death (Romans 6:23) and destruction (1 Corinthians 3:17). Peter also used such language (2 Peter 2), likening the destruction of the ungodly to the burning of Sodom and Gomorrah. And John anticipated the wicked being consumed in the lake of fire, which he called "the second death" (Revelation 20:14, 15).

Whatever its appeal, the annihilationist position contains substantive problems. One is the biblical assertions that the wicked will suffer an "eternal" fate. Annihilationists argue that the word eternal refers to the permanence of the results of judgment and not to the duration of the act of punishment. Many Scripture passages, however, say more than this. Biblical writers use the word eternal to refer not only to the punishment of the lost but also to the bliss of the righteous (Matthew 25:46), suggesting a parallel that goes beyond the permanence of the pronounced judgment. The unending joy of the redeemed stands in contrast to the unending torment of the reprobate.

> Doesn't passing out of existence trivialize the seriousness of the choices we make in life and the importance of our response to God's loving offer of community?

Also, several New Testament texts indicate that the lost will suffer varying degrees of punishment. Jesus declared that those who have received greater opportunities for belief will suffer more severe condemnation (Matthew 10:15; 11:20-24; Luke 12:47, 48). While many annihilationists believe in different degrees of torment before extinction, they anticipate only one ultimate destiny for all the wicked, an undifferentiated nonexistence. But can a righteous Judge pronounce the same sentence of destiny upon the most despicable villain of human history as upon the seemingly moral pagan? Also, doesn't passing out of existence trivialize the seriousness of the choices we make in life and the importance of our response to God's loving offer of community?

In sum, yes, some evangelical theologians affirm annihilationism, but it is important to keep in mind that annihilationists affirm several aspects of the traditional view. This issue, therefore, should not be lumped in with the more substantial debate over universalism, which denies a final judgment altogether. The debate raised by annihilationists reminds us of the diffi-culties that arise whenever we attempt to pinpoint the eternal situation of the lost. Just as we cannot envision what conscious bliss will mean to the saved in their resurrection bodies, so also we do not know exactly what eternal punishment will be like. Finally, the controversy surrounding the nature of eternal dam-nation will serve a positive purpose if it leads us to realize that we ought never to speak about the fate of the lost without tears in our eyes.

Stanley J. Grenz was professor of theology at Carey/Regent College in Vancouver, British Columbia, Canada, and the author of numerous books. "Is Hell Forever?" was first published in the October 1998 issue of Christianity Today.

LAUNCH

OPTIONAL EXERCISE

Your group may want to begin your meeting with this activity. Someone will need to bring **pens, index cards,** and a silly **prize** (optional).

Each group member should get an index card and a pen. Spread out around the room so you each have some private space. Now, in just a few sentences, write a description of your most embarrassing moment. Make sure you don't write your name on your card.

Gather back together and choose one person to collect all the cards, shuffle them, and then read them aloud one by one. Try to guess who you think the author is behind each embarrassing moment.

At the end, vote together and select the most hilarious moment. If you want, award a prize to the winner of the funniest embarrassing moment (such as a plastic Groucho Marx mustache-and-nose-and-glasses combo for when that person has to go out in public).

After the laughter subsides, discuss these questions: Which aspects of Christianity can be embarrassing for you to talk about with others? What features of church culture do you think seem kooky to the rest of the world?

When's the last time you heard a sermon on Hell? It's not the church's favorite topic. We tend to downplay it in our evangelism resources, choosing rather to focus on spending eternity in Heaven with God. It's almost like Hell is an embarrassment—like it's a bad marketing idea or something. It's no wonder then, that unorthodox ideas like universalism can creep into some Christians' thinking. Universalism is the belief that all people will eventually somehow be saved. Or there's annihilationism, which some argue still fits within the bounds of Christian orthodoxy. Annihilationism posits that, rather than suffering eternally in Hell (the traditional view), souls are wiped from existence either immediately at death, after a time of punishment, or at the final judgment.

1 How do you feel about discussing Hell with non-Christians? Embarrassed? Awkward? Apologetic? Excited? Confident? Explain.

2 At first glance, does annihilationism seem more "fair" to you than eternal punishment? Why or why not?

ENGAGE

ETERNAL DESTRUCTION FROM AN ANNIHILATIONIST VIEWPOINT

You probably grew up with only one version of Hell: hot and forever. The annihilationist position, however, challenges our Sunday-school foundations and the way we read Scripture. Theologian J. I. Packer clarifies the issue:

> The question is essentially exegetical, though with theological and pastoral implications. It boils down to whether, when Jesus said that those banished at the final judgment will "go away into eternal punishment" (Matthew 25:46), He envisaged a state of penal pain that is endless, or an ending of conscious existence that is irrevocable: that is ... a punishment that is eternal in its length or in its effect. Mainstream Christianity has always affirmed the former, and still does; evangelical annihilationists ... affirm the latter.[1]

Annihilationists draw upon the following key Bible passages which portray God's destruction of those who are wicked or who do not believe. Examine the following passages to help you better understand the annihilationist perspective. Take notes in the space provided, recording your key observations about what these passages say regarding death, destruction, Hell, and the afterlife.

Read **Psalm 37; Malachi 4:1-5; Matthew 3:10-12; Matthew 10:28; Romans 6:23;** and **1 Corinthians 3:17.** Write your thoughts in the space provided.

1 Imagine your understanding of Hell was based *only* on what you've read here. How would you define or describe it? Why?

2 Do you allow for, or have more sympathy for, the annihilationist position after reading these passages? Why or why not?

3 How might someone with a traditional view of Hell understand and interpret these verses? Explain.

ETERNAL DESCRIBES BOTH PUNISHMENT AND REWARD

The traditional Christian view of Hell is a place or state of ongoing punishment. It's hard to swallow, but read Jesus' descriptions of Hell in **Matthew 25:41-46** and **Mark 9:42-48.**

4

How would you describe Hell after reading these passages? How do they add to or influence your interpretation of the destruction-oriented passages you read earlier?

DELVE DEEPER

If you'd like, explore this question as a group or on your own:

Grenz pointed out that the doctrine of annihilation came about after the Reformation. The debate has seen a recent resurgence in evangelicalism in part due to theologian John R. W. Stott's allowance for the doctrine in a book called *Evangelical Essentials*. He wrote:

> Emotionally, I find the concept [of eternal conscious torment] intolerable and do not understand how people can live with it without either cauterizing their feelings or cracking under the strain. But our emotions are a fluctuating, unreliable guide to truth and must not be exalted to the place of supreme authority in determining it . . . my question must be—and is—not what does my heart tell me, but what does God's Word say?[2]

What do you think about Stott's statements here? Do you resonate with his perspective? What may be changing in our culture (or in our church culture) that has led to the recent rekindling of this debate? Why do you think annihilationism is finding a more sympathetic audience in the church today than during other times?

What did Jesus mean when he said "the fire *never* goes out," "*eternal* fire," and "*eternal* punishment" (emphasis added)? Annihilationists assert that the word *eternal* in passages such as these speaks of an eternally permanent result rather than an ongoing length of time. But in his *Christianity Today* article, Grenz pointed out that "biblical writers use the word *eternal* to refer not only to the punishment of the lost but also to the bliss of the righteous (Matthew 25:46), suggesting a parallel that goes beyond the permanence of the pronounced judgment. The unending joy of the redeemed stands in contrast to the unending torment of the reprobate." In other words, *eternal* must logically mean the same thing when it's used in Scripture to describe both Heaven and Hell.

5 In your opinion, how does Jesus' parallel use of the word *eternal* here affect the debate?

6 What does Hell defined by eternal (in duration) punishment tell you about God's holiness? about his kingdom? about sin? Explain.

THE REALITY OF HELL SHOULD BRING TEARS TO OUR EYES

Although it may be a minority view, annihilationism has some well-known evangelical sympathizers and adherents. It's important to remember that annihilationists don't dismiss the reality of a final judgment, as universalists do.

Read **Revelation 20:7-15**.

7 What does this passage contribute to the traditionalism vs. annihilationism debate?

8 Based on this passage and the others you've read, what do you imagine Jesus might say to Christians today about the way we communicate the reality of sin, judgment, and Hell? Explain.

Grenz concluded his assessment of annihilationism by writing, "The controversy surrounding the nature of eternal damnation will serve a positive purpose if it leads us to realize that we ought never to speak about the fate of the lost without tears in our eyes."

 9 Do you grieve over the fate of the lost? Why or why not?

 10 In light of all you've studied and discussed, what's your conclusion about this controversy? Can annihilationism fit within the bounds of Christian orthodoxy? Explain your reasoning.

RESPOND

Imagine a close Christian friend of yours finds it too difficult to stomach the idea of Hell as eternal torture and pain. Your friend is considering adopting the annihilationist view and wants to know what you think. What would you say to your friend? What ideas would you share? What questions might you ask him or her?

DELVE DEEPER

If you'd like, explore this question as a group or on your own:

Grenz asked this question: "[D]oesn't passing out of existence trivialize the seriousness of the choices we make in life and the importance of our response to God's loving offer of community?"

Having considered the judgment scene in Revelation 20, how might a belief in annihilationism (let alone universalism) impact evangelism? If you believed that your nonbelieving loved ones would simply cease to exist, would you be as motivated to share your faith? Explain.

REACT

During this study, how has God challenged you personally in regard to the doctrine of Hell and the debate between traditionalists and annihilationists? What's one step you will take to respond to God's Word in this area? Jot down your thoughts in the space below.

Take time as a group to pray for those you know who are "lost." Go around your circle and pray for compassion and intentionality when it comes to sharing your faith with non-Christian family members, friends, and neighbors.

FOR FURTHER STUDY

BOOKS/ANNIHILATIONISM

- *Evangelical Essentials: A Liberal-Evangelical Dialogue* by David L. Edwards and John Stott (InterVarsity)
- *The Fire That Consumes* by Edward Fudge (Paternoster)
- *The True Image: The Origin and Destiny of Man in Christ* by Philip E. Hughes (Eerdmans)
- "The Case for Conditional Immortality" by John W. Wenham, *Universalism and the Doctrine of Hell* (Baker)

BOOKS/TRADITIONALISM

- *Evangelical Affirmations* by Kenneth Kantzer and Carl Henry, eds. (Academie)
- *Hell on Trial* by Robert A. Peterson (Presbyterian & Reformed)
- *The Gagging of God: Christianity Confronts Pluralism* by D. A. Carson (Zondervan)
- *Repent or Perish* by John H. Gerstner (Soli Deo Gloria)

ONLINE ARTICLES

- "Evangelical Annihilationism in Review" by J. I. Packer from *Reformation & Revival* (www.the-highway.com/annihilationism_Packer.html)
- "Undying Worm, Unquenchable Fire" by Robert A. Peterson from *Christianity Today* (www.christianitytoday.com/ct/2000/october23/1.30.html)

STRETCH

Set aside some time soon after your small group meeting to think and pray about the nature of Hell and our responsibility toward the lost.

Consider this claim from the book *A is for Abductive:*

Lost has become something of a technical term in recent years to refer to unsaved, unbelieving, unconverted, and otherwise non-Christian people. True and helpful phrases like "lost people matter to God" have popularized this usage. . . . Meanwhile, there is reason to ask, Who is really lost, them or us? Consider an analogy. When a letter is sent, and it never arrives at its intended destination, we say it is lost. Similarly, Christians have been sent into the world . . . as a kind of love letter from God to all. Yet few of us have actually arrived with our message in the world to which we have been sent. Perhaps we would be wiser to refer to *ourselves* as the lost.[3]

Questions to ponder:

- What's your reaction to this observation about evangelism? Is there any truth to it? Why or why not?

- Which Scripture passages most affected you from your small group study? Why?
- Re-read Revelation 20:7-15. As you consider these images of Hell, think for a moment about the eternal destiny of those around you. Who in your life needs to hear the good news from you? What conversations do you need to begin? What's holding you back?

Take time to pray for a renewed compassion for the lost; pray specifically for friends and loved ones who came to mind as you pondered Revelation 20:7-15.

Study written by Kyle White. Kyle is the founding director of Neighbors' House, an outreach to at-risk students in DeKalb County, Illinois. He is a freelance writer, frequent contributor to ChristianBibleStudies.com, and the author of *Wisconsin River of Grace*.

WHAT IS HEAVEN?
{ SEEING HEAVEN MORE CLEARLY, AND WHY IT MATTERS }

Before you meet with your small group, read this good question.
Then read the response article written by Arthur O. Roberts.

GQ 4 **Where is Heaven and how will we experience it before the final resurrection?**

One popular view locates heaven in a separate, non-material world. In recent centuries, scientists and clergy seemed to strike a bargain: science gets the body (and other physical substances) while religion gets the soul (and other non-material stuff). Social scientists claimed title to the psyche, however, leaving the church a wispy, anemic, spiritual realm congenial to neither scientific nor biblical insights about creation and human nature.

This view sidesteps the physicality of Jesus' incarnation and resurrection and their implications about heaven. It lacks the full force of the Christian hope for personal, conscious life after death.

Heaven is located within creation. It isn't tucked into a galactic corner. Rather, we can experience glimpses of heaven through ordinary senses, reason, and intuition. Heaven is behind us, among us, around us, within us, before us—eventually to be fully experienced eternally in our resurrection bodies. Heaven is as real as oceans and suns, winds and planets in a hundred billion whirling galaxies. It is as real as people with bodies, minds, and spirits.

We find intimations of heaven in stories of humankind, spiritual experiences, and nature, but in Scripture we get our fullest picture: The triumph of Christ over dark powers will release the cosmos from sin's bondage (Romans 8:21). On the Last Day, we will become more, not less, embodied (note the highly physical description of heaven in Revelation 21). Heaven is a dimension in which the cosmos is bathed in holiness (Revelation 21:22-27).

Heaven is where Jesus is.

The apostle Peter understood Jesus' promise, "I go to prepare a place for you" (John 14:2, NRSV), to mean not only his presence now but also a heavenly life with him. The present universe, Peter said, will be reconstituted—"a new heaven and a new earth, the home of righteousness" (2 Peter 3:13). The apostle Paul pictured the "whole creation" groaning like a woman in labor. Those having the "firstfruits of the Spirit" eagerly anticipated bodily redemption and sharing the glory of the risen Lord (Romans 8:15-25).

In heaven, cultures from this world will be shaped toward divine purposes (Revelation 21:24). But for all these intimations, heaven is a place we simply cannot fully imagine yet: "No eye has seen, no ear has heard, no mind has conceived what God has prepared for those who love him" (1 Corinthians 2:9).

What form will we have before the final resurrection? Even with his vision of "a man in Christ" who was caught up in "the third heaven," the apostle Paul did not know whether it was in or out of the body—"God knows," he wrote (2 Corinthians 12:2-4). Nor do we know whether this vision refers to a state after the final resurrection. But we do know from Paul that, on the last day, we will bear the likeness of Jesus: "And just as we have borne the likeness of the earthly man, so shall we bear the likeness of the man from heaven" (1 Corinthians 15:49).

We may take our cue from Jesus. Jesus' triumph over death signals our own victory. Jesus is first through the mountain pass, as it were. Death isn't the last word; life is—personal, conscious continuation beyond death. In post-resurrection mode, he moved between two dimensions. As earthly "children of the resurrection," we access one dimension of the kingdom of God in this life; in heaven we'll experience a new dimension of it, though still awaiting our glorified bodies. We will be with the risen Jesus (Philippians 1:23), and therefore we will be of some essence or form to perceive and reflect his likeness.

> Death isn't the last word; life is—personal, conscious continuation beyond death.

The dead in Christ aren't in limbo awaiting the end-time melding of modes. Given the relativity of time, in relation to us, they're already enjoying some form of the New Jerusalem. This "great cloud of witnesses" (Greek: "martyrs") hovers about us, mind touching mind, spirit touching spirit, and one day, at the final resurrection of the Last Day, hand grasping hand! Created in the image of God, in the new heaven and earth we will put on God's likeness. As John wrote: "Beloved, we are God's children now; what we will be has not yet been revealed. What we do know is this: when he is revealed, we will be like him, for we will see him as he is. And all who have *this hope in him purify themselves, just as he is pure" (1 John 3:2, 3, NRSV).*

Heaven is where Jesus is; and after death some form of ourselves, reflecting the risen Jesus, will function in dimensions of reality not now accessible to us.

Arthur O. Roberts is professor-at-large at George Fox University and author of Exploring Heaven: What Great Christian Thinkers Tell Us About Our Afterlife with God. *"Finding Heaven" was first published in the April 2005 issue of* Christianity Today.

LAUNCH

OPTIONAL EXERCISE

Your group may want to begin your meeting with this activity. You'll need **pens** and **slips of paper** (one per participant) as well as a **flip-chart or whiteboard** and **marker**.

First, each person should take a slip of paper and write a word or phrase on it that is associated with Heaven. Draw upon ideas and images in Revelation 21 or use some of these words and phrases: streets of gold, holy city, throne of God, temple, gate of Heaven, bride, Lamb's book of life, water of life, thirsty, measuring rod. Fold up all the papers and put them in a pile.

Next, form two equally sized teams to play a game that mixes charades and Pictionary. Take turns drawing a slip of paper. Each player can choose between acting out the phrase or drawing it while the rest of his or her team makes guesses. If that player's team isn't able to guess correctly within thirty seconds, the other team gets a chance to guess. Award one point for each correct answer.

People have all kinds of misconceptions about Heaven. These myths are popularized in movies, television, books, and even jokes. The Bible, however, provides a very different picture of Heaven than what our culture portrays.

1 What are some examples of misconceptions or myths about Heaven you've observed in our culture? Where did you see or hear them?

2 Which of the words below best matches how you pictured Heaven when you were a child or teenager? How has your view of Heaven changed over the years?
- Boring
- Bright
- Cloudy
- Unimaginable
- Nonexistent

ENGAGE

GOD HAS PROVIDED A NEW PLACE FOR HIS PEOPLE IN HEAVEN

The story of human history begins in Genesis and ends in Revelation. And in both instances, at the beginning and the end, God is creating.

Read **Revelation 21:1-4.**

Genesis 1:1 says, "In the beginning, God created the heavens and the earth." At the beginning of Revelation 21, God creates "a new heaven and a new earth." Look at the comparison below of other parallels found in Genesis and Revelation. (If you'd like, look up these passages in your Bible.)

Genesis	Revelation
1:5 God establishes night	22:5 No night in the new creation
1:16 God creates the sun	21:23 No need for the sun
1:10 God creates the seas	21:1 No more seas
3:6 Sin enters the human race	21:27 No more sin
3:8 Humans hide from God	21:3 God invites people into his presence
3:16, 17 Humankind is cursed	22:3 No more curse
3:17 Suffering begins	21:4 No more suffering
3:19 Death initiated	21:4 No more death
3:24 Humankind driven from paradise	22:14 Humans are restored to paradise

1 What's your reaction to these comparisons? What stands out to you about the way God brings to completion (in Revelation 21–22) what he began in Genesis 1–3? Explain.

Read **Revelation 21:5-8.** This passage describes the event that Jesus called the "renewal of all things" in Matthew 19:28.

2 What hope do you think the phrase "I am making everything new!" gave to the persecuted Christians in the first century (the original recipients of Revelation) or to Christians throughout the ages? What hope can followers today receive from these verses?

In his *Christianity Today* article, Arthur O. Roberts asserts that Heaven is a very real place located within creation, rather than in a separate, non-material world. He says, "Heaven is as real as oceans and suns, winds and planets in a hundred billion whirling galaxies. It is as real as people with bodies, minds, and spirits."

3 Is the idea that Heaven is a real place important to your faith? Why or why not?

DELVE DEEPER

If you'd like, explore this question as a group or on your own:

Read Revelation 21:9-21. This section provides a very detailed description of the Holy City, the New Jerusalem. The dimensions are staggering! If taken literally, the city is fifteen-hundred miles square, composed of 396,000 stories (at twenty feet per story), and each measuring about half the size of the United States![1]

All these specifications are symbols, meant to help us *imagine* what Heaven will be like. What words would you use to describe your future eternal home?

To comfort his followers (including us), Jesus promised that he would go to his "Father's house" to prepare a place for them (and us). Read **John 14:1-4**.

4 If you had been one of those listening to Jesus, what would have comforted you the most about his Father's house? Explain.

GOD IS PRESENT WITH HIS PEOPLE IN HEAVEN

German philosopher and critic of Christianity Friedrich Nietzsche once said, "In heaven all interesting men are missing."[2] While some may find this quote provocative or amusing, others probably find his cynicism quite sad. There *are* some things that will be missing in Heaven; earlier in Revelation 21, we saw some things that will not be in the new Heaven and earth such as death, mourning, crying, and pain, because the old order of things has passed away (21:4). But there are a few more important things that will be missing as well.

5 Read **Revelation 21:22-27**. What does John say we will *not* find in the Holy City? Why is this significant? What will take their place?

6 Since Heaven is God's dwelling place, we will be with him there for the rest of eternity. Re-read **Revelation 21:3-7.** What descriptions do you see in these verses of the personal relationship we will have with God in our eternal home?

In his book *Heaven*, Randy Alcorn writes, "When we're told in Revelation 22:4 that we'll see God's face, it should astound us. For this to happen, it would require that we undergo something radical between now and then. . . . Not only will we see his face and live, but we will likely wonder if we ever lived before we saw his face! To see God will be our greatest joy, the joy by which all others will be measured."[3]

It is impossible, even unimaginable to some, to see God's face and live before the renewal of all things (see 1 Timothy 6:16; Hebrews 12:14), and yet, Jesus said, "Blessed are the pure in heart, for they will see God" (Matthew 5:8). Today we can approach God's throne in prayer with confidence because of the blood of Jesus (see Hebrews 4:16; 10:19). Now, as imperfect but forgiven people, Paul says, "we see but

DELVE DEEPER

If you'd like, explore this question as a group or on your own:

We will find rest in Heaven (see Revelation 14:13 and Hebrews 4:10, 11), but there will also be fulfilling work to do there. In the original Eden, before the curse, God put the man in the garden to take care of it and work in it. In the new Heaven and new earth, humans will likely be given work to do as well. Teacher and author Sean McDowell writes, "But this is not work as we often experience it today. There will not be pressing deadlines, stressful co-workers, homework assignments, or bitter competition. Rather, we will feel truly fulfilled because we will work in a manner fitting to the way God has designed each of us. The pain, corruption, and sin that tarnish work today will be gone forever. We will be free to work for the benefit of God, others, and ourselves."[4]

How do you think the work we will do in Heaven compares or contrasts with your work in the world today?

a poor reflection as in a mirror," but when perfection comes in the form of the new Heaven and new earth, "we shall see face to face" (1 Corinthians 13:12)!

 7 What do you imagine it will be like to see God's face? What does it mean to you to see and be seen by God?

GOD HAS A PURPOSE FOR HEAVEN

The last chapter of our Bible encourages us with an image of what we will be doing in eternity and it teaches us what we should be doing now as we await the new Heaven and new earth.

Arthur O. Roberts says, "In heaven, cultures from this world will be shaped toward divine purposes." Read **Revelation 22:1-9.**

 8 From this passage and what you've read in Revelation 21, what are some of the things we'll do for all eternity?

9 Unlike the garden paradise in Genesis 1, Revelation describes Heaven as a bustling city. With this urban motif in mind, what other activities do you imagine we may do in Heaven (though they may not be mentioned specifically in Revelation)? Explain.

Read **Revelation 22:10-21.** Commentator Warren Wiersbe said about this passage, "Heaven is more than a destination. It's a motivation."[5]

10 How is this true for you? What does the hope of Heaven motivate you to do in this life?

RESPOND

An old cliché goes, "Don't be so heavenly minded that you are no earthly good." Do you agree or disagree with this statement? Why? (Defend your answer!)

REACT

Think through these questions and then jot your thoughts down in the space provided: During this study, how has God challenged your understanding of Heaven? What's one step you will take to be prepared to say, "Come, Lord Jesus" (Revelation 22:20)? How might you help someone else to make that preparation?

FOR FURTHER STUDY
BOOKS

- *The Divine Conspiracy* by Dallas Willard (HarperSanFrancisco)
- *The Glory of Heaven* by John MacArthur (Crossway)
- *A Grief Observed* by C. S. Lewis (Bantam Books)
- *Heaven* by Randy Alcorn (Tyndale)
- *Heaven: Your Real Home* by Joni Eareckson Tada (Zondervan)
- *One Minute After You Die* by Erwin W. Lutzer (Moody Press)

ONLINE ARTICLES

- "Heaven: God's Highest Hope," by Max Lucado (www.maxlucado.com/pdf/heaven.gods.highest.hope.pdf)
- "What Will Heaven Be Like?" by Sean McDowell from Worldview Ministries (www.seanmcdowell.org/media/articles/theology/heaven.asp)

AUDIO RESOURCES

- *Finally Home* MP3 Audio Series by Max Lucado (www.maxlucado.net/_catalog_30321/Finally_Home)
- "I Can Only Imagine" by Mercy Me
- "How Far Is Heaven?" by Los Lonely Boys, popularized by Salvador
- "There Will Be a Day" by Jeremy Camp
- "I Will Rise" by Chris Tomlin
- "Streets of Gold" by NeedtoBreathe
- "No Earthly Good" by Johnny Cash

Form mini-groups of three to four and spend time praying together. Take turns praying aloud for each of the others in your group, asking God to work in each other's lives as you seek to live in a way today that embodies your future hope of Heaven.

STRETCH

Studying Heaven and thinking about someday seeing God face-to-face should compel us to worship him like never before! Take time this week to engage in at least one of the following activities as an act of worship:

1. Listen to one of the songs listed in For Further Study and allow it to lead you into worship.

2. Read the account of worship around the throne in Heaven in Revelation 4. Use the worship of the four living creatures as a template for your own time of worshipping God.

3. Take a walk outside if you can, taking time to notice the beauty of God's creation around you. Leave your cell phone ringer turned off, and take only a pad of paper and pen with you. Stop and write words of praise to God for his creation.

4. Share with someone who is not in your small group what you have learned about Heaven and discuss the implications of living for eternity.

5. Meditate on Colossians 3:1-4. Make it your theme verse this week. Memorize it. Ask God to show you what you should set your mind on this week. Journal your thoughts, prayers, and what you hear from God as he responds to you.

6. How can you serve God this week: within your church family, in your community, or even in your own home? "Whatever you do, work at it with all your heart, as working for the Lord, not for men" (Colossians 3:23). Focus on one specific response of service—then do it!

Study written by Michael Mack. Michael is a small groups pastor and is the founder of SmallGroups.com and SmallGroupLeadership.com. He has written numerous books about small group leadership, including *I'm a Leader . . . Now What?* (Standard Publishing).

WHAT DO WE GAIN FROM BODILY RESURRECTION?
{ NEW BODIES, RENEWED HOPE }

PREPARE

Before you meet with your small group, read this good question. Then read the response article written by Timothy George.

GQ 5 If after death we are already in the joy of God's presence, **what exactly do we gain from a bodily resurrection?**

The world in which Christianity arose affirmed the immortality of the soul, a cornerstone of Greek philosophy. Platonic arguments for the soul's innate immortality have influenced views about life after death from Gnosticism to the New Age movement today. The soul's immortality was a central tenet in Kant's philosophy and this was echoed in the triad of Protestant liberalism—the fatherhood of God, the brotherhood of man, and the immortality of the soul.

But biblical faith has always insisted on something very different. God's ultimate purpose for all his human creatures, for the lost as well as for the redeemed (John 5:29; Acts 24:15), is not an eternal, incorporeal existence but rather the resurrection of the body. This concept has been offensive to human reason from the beginning, as Paul found out when he

preached about Jesus and the Resurrection to the philoso-
phers of Mars Hill (Acts 17:22-34).

Yet belief in the bodily resurrection is so basic that it was
included in the Apostles' Creed.

Why make such a fuss about the body? Because of three
key moments in the history of salvation: Creation, Incarnation,
and Redemption.

When God first created the material world, and human
beings within it from the dust of the earth, he pronounced
his work "very good." God did not create human beings as
ghost-like creatures but as embodied souls. The resurrection
of the body affirms the goodness of God's original creation,
and recognizes that the basic human problem is not finitude
but fallenness. It also declares that God will make good and
bring to perfection the human project he began in the Garden
of Eden.

The Incarnation teaches that the eternal Son of God entered so deeply into our human reality that he did not shun
the virgin's womb, nor the evildoer's cross. This same one,
Jesus Christ, also rose again in his body "on the third day."

Jesus' bodily resurrection is the guarantee of our own future resurrection. He rose literally, physically, historically, and
in a body that was no less visible and tangible than those of
his very earthly disciples, though remarkably transformed
nonetheless. All of this gives us reason to hope that "when
he appears, we shall be like him, for we shall see him as he is"
(1 John 3:2). Despite the persistence of sin, death, and decay,
we can live with confidence and hope that God's Kingdom
will indeed come in a way that ends these miseries.

At Jesus' second coming, God will complete the restoration work he has already begun. He will redeem our bodies as well as our souls. Indeed, the entire cosmos will be gathered up in a new unity—that is, an ultimate healing, reconciliation, and bringing together of all things in Christ (Ephesians 1:10).

What will our resurrection bodies be like? This question was already asked in 1 Corinthians 15:35. God does not give us a complete answer, but we do know that our new, glorified bodies will be imperishable. No more cancer, no more drownings, no more holocausts.

Our bodies will also be spiritual (Greek, pneumatikos). This word does not mean nonphysical, but rather bodies "transformed by and adopted to the new world of God's Spirit" (George E. Ladd). They also will be recognizable, but, like Jesus' risen body, so utterly transformed that we shall be aware of the differences as well as the sameness.

> At Jesus' second coming, God will complete the restoration work he has already begun.

Most Christians believe that between death and the resurrection we shall indeed live in God's presence in conscious awareness of the Lord and others who have gone before us. This is wonderful, but it is not the end of the journey. In some ways, it is only the prelude to the main event that will begin in earnest on "that great getting-up morning" and that will include the new heavens and the new earth, the marriage banquet of the Lamb, the de-fanging of Satan, and the abolition of sin and sorrow forever.

Timothy George is Dean of Beeson Divinity School of Samford University and an executive editor of Christianity Today. "Heavenly Bodies" was first published in the February 2003 issue of Christianity Today.

LAUNCH

OPTIONAL EXERCISE

Your group may want to begin your meeting with this activity. You'll need **paper** and **colored pencils, crayons,** or **markers.**

The word *eschatological* refers to final or last things. Perhaps, before you began this study, you had some specific ideas about what last things you would experience in—and after—death. Think about how you've imagined this. Most of us have been influenced in specific ways about our hope for the future. Maybe childhood stories about Heaven, films about the end-times, or scary Hell-and-damnation sermons have influenced how you think about Christian eschatology. Reflect on these experiences, then draw a picture or write out specific words in creative ways to describe your thoughts about the end-times.

When everyone is finished, look at the pictures and words together. Try to categorize the ideas about the future by making several piles of related pictures and words. Make up a name for each category such as "Heavenly Roads" or "Choirs of Souls." Once the images and words are categorized, put the categories in an order from "absolutely sure it will happen" to "speculative and iffy at best."

You can tell a lot about people's eschatological beliefs by how they talk at funerals and memorial services. When a young athlete tragically died, for example, mourners at his Christian funeral said things like, "He's in Heaven right now skateboarding down those streets of gold" and "He loved God so much he ran up to him and gave him a hug."

1 What presumptions about death and the body do these comments demonstrate?

2 How have you envisioned Christians you know who have died? Have you ever thought about what they might be doing now? What do you think about that?

ENGAGE

THE RESURRECTION IS A BIBLICAL REALITY

Often, when Christians speak about their eschatological hope, they speak about going to Heaven when they die. Yes, this is certainly part of the Christian hope, but it is by no means the whole story. One of the differences between Christianity and most other religions is that Christianity

DELVE DEEPER

If you'd like, explore this question as a group or on your own:

How do we know that the resurrection of the body isn't instantaneous at death? How do we know that the deceased believers aren't already up in Heaven with their resurrected bodies?

Well, we know this because of the example of Jesus. The first indicator of Jesus' resurrection was the empty tomb. There was no body, because his body had been resurrected. If the bodies of Christians disappeared after death, we could believe in a sort of instantaneous resurrection—but that's not the case. Most of us have seen the deceased bodies of loved ones lying in a coffin. It's understanding the finality of death that makes the resurrection such a glorious hope.

Read Paul's discussion of death, the body, and being in Christ's presence in Philippians 1:18-26.

What's your understanding of the way the timing of all this works out? How might the difference between our human understanding of time and God's eternal reality outside of time impact the way we read and understand Scriptures about bodily resurrection, Heaven, and the end-times?

teaches the bodily resurrection of the dead. This resurrection is not something that happens when someone dies; it's something that will happen to all of us in the future kingdom. So, even when a believer dies, we can say that he or she is with God (see Philippians 1:18-26) but the resurrection—the final, hopeful event—has not yet occurred. Sadly, however, the resurrection of the dead is not often discussed in churches or even at Christian funerals.

This is not new to the contemporary church. During the time of the early church, Paul's message of the resurrection of the dead seemed to be falling upon deaf ears, especially in the church of Corinth. **1 Corinthians 15** communicates some of Paul's frustrations with this church's beliefs. Choose someone in your group with a good dramatic voice to read this chapter aloud.

 1 Go back through the passage and together list the issues Paul addressed regarding the resurrection of the dead. Based on Paul's comments, what sorts of conversations do you think were going on in the church in Corinth regarding the resurrection?

 2 Are these questions you have, as well? Explain.

3 How has the discussion about the resurrection changed over the years? How has it remained the same?

4 How can Paul's metaphor of the sown seed help us to understand the future resurrection? Explain.

THE BODY IS PART OF BEING MADE IN GOD'S IMAGE

Read **Genesis 1:26, 27**. As Timothy George points out, human beings are embodied souls, not "ghost-like creatures." What's important to know in the story of God's creation of humanity is that the body is a significant and valuable part of what it is to be human and what it means to be made in God's image. (This is not meant to imply that God has a body. Consider the metaphor of a painter painting a self-portrait. It is an image of himself, but that does not mean that he is two-dimensional and made of oil paints and canvas. We have to understand that God is much too big a being for us to begin to comprehend!)

In the ancient Near East, the concept of an image was a "representative of one who is really spiritually present, though physically absent," such as a king who would put his statue on conquered territory. Biblical scholar D. J. A. Clines explains, "The body is not a mere dwelling-place for the soul, nor is it the prison-house of the soul. Insofar as man is a body and a bodiless man is not man, the body is the image of God; for man is the image of God. Man is the flesh-and-blood image of the invisible God."[1]

5 How have you understood what it means to be made in God's image? Has the human body been part of your understanding? Why or why not?

6 Like an Ancient Near-Eastern statue or image on a coin, we who are made in God's image are to represent God himself. What difference would it make in your everyday life if you more purposefully thought of yourself as a "representative of one [God] who is really spiritually present, though physically absent"? Give examples.

Historically, being created in God's image has meant various things to different theologians and biblical scholars. Primary views have included the *substantive view*, which simply has to do with specific traits that both humanity and God have (such as reason, will, intellect, and moral nature); the *relational view*, which focuses on the use of the word *us* in Genesis 1:26 (where the Holy Trinity, who is in relationship with one another, creates humanity for relationships); and the *functional view*, which links the image of God to the vocational role of ruling over the earth (as in Genesis 1:26).[2]

But when we incorporate the human body into our understanding of what it means to be made in God's image, we can affirm all of these other viewpoints—substantive, relational, and functional. For instance, one could not care for creation, be married, or act in a moral way without a body.

7 How does understanding the physical implications of being made in God's image affect your perspective on bodily resurrection? What new significance or meaning does it add? Explain.

BELIEF IN BODILY RESURRECTION IS ESSENTIAL TO FAITH

Sometimes negative perspectives about the body can creep into the church. For example, there's the idea that the physical body is where sin and decay lie and, without the physical body, we would be better—more holy, perhaps. This perspective has its roots in Gnosticism, a belief system influenced by Greek culture that also began to creep into the early church. Within the Gnostic worldview, "The material creation, including the body, was regarded as inherently evil." Eschatological hope, for the Gnostics, was "to escape from the prison of their bodies at death and to traverse the planetary spheres of hostile demons to be reunited with God."[3] Their hope had nothing at all to do with the resurrection. In fact, because their primary goal was to escape the body, they completely rejected the idea of the resurrection.

DELVE DEEPER

If you'd like, explore this question as a group or on your own:

Christ's incarnation demonstrates the value of the human body. John 1, one of the most complicated and beautiful texts in the New Testament, speaks to us about the incarnation of Christ. Read John 1:1-18.

In Timothy George's article, he explains that, "The Incarnation teaches that the eternal Son of God entered so deeply into our human reality that he did not shun the virgin's womb, nor the evildoer's cross. This same one, Jesus Christ, also rose again in his body 'on the third day.'" It's important to remember the humanity of Jesus: that he grew and was born the way all babies are born. Jesus had all the bodily functions we do. He probably got sick. He used the bathroom. He went through puberty.

Do you tend to think of Jesus as more man or more God? How difficult is it for you to remain balanced in your understanding of the incarnation? How can the reality of the incarnation strengthen your understanding of the resurrection? Explain.

8 What are some modern-day examples of the Gnostic tendency to venerate the soul over the body? Does this happen often in contemporary culture or in the church today? Explain.

Together, read **Acts 17:16-34** aloud.

9 Considering what you just learned about the Gnostic tradition, how radical is Paul's speech? How does this scenario compare and contrast with what it's like to assert belief in Jesus' resurrection and the final resurrection in our culture today?

10 Do you think what one believes about the body and the idea of a final resurrection really matters on a practical, day-to-day level? Why or why not?

RESPOND

What would you say to a Christian friend who said that the resurrection of the dead wasn't really an issue that mattered, and that sometimes she understood why people believed in reincarnation? What would you say if this friend was not a believer?

REACT

For a moment, think about how you view your own body. Do you think of it as something to be discarded in the future? Do you worship it? Do you abhor it? Consider how a renewed vision of the resurrection of the dead can help you to understand how God views your body. How can this influence your attitude and actions? What does it mean to live as a person who will one day be raised from the dead? Privately write your thoughts below.

Once everyone has considered these questions, gather in a group and take turns praying aloud, asking God to help you remember the resurrection and the stories he has given us that demonstrate his love of humanity and his choice to make us embodied.

FOR FURTHER STUDY

BOOKS

- *Incarnation* by Alister McGrath (Fortress Press)
- *Incarnation and Resurrection* by Paul D. Molnar (Eerdmans)
- *Surprised by Hope* by N. T. Wright (Harper One)
- *Raised with Christ: How the Resurrection Changes Everything* by Adrian Warnock (Crossway)
- *The Resurrection of the Son of God* by N. T. Wright (Fortress Press)

ONLINE ARTICLES

- "The Empty Tomb and the Empty Urn" by Russell D. Moore, from *Christianity Today* (www.ctlibrary.com/ct/2009/april web-only/114-21.0.html)
- "A Resurrection That Matters" by J. R. Daniel Kirk, from *Christianity Today* (www.christianitytoday.com/ct/2010/april/10.37.html)

SONGS AND POETRY

- *Accompanied by Angels: Poems of the Incarnation* by Luci Shaw (Eerdmans)
- *A Widening Light: Poems of the Incarnation* by Luci Shaw, ed. (Regent College Publishing)
- "On the Mystery of the Incarnation" by Denise Levertov (famouspoetsand poems.com/poets/denise_levertov/poems/18663)

STRETCH

Set aside some time for yourself in the following week for contemplation of Scripture through a musical interpretation of the resurrection.

Listen to "The trumpet shall sound" from Handel's *Messiah*. (If you don't have a copy of *Messiah*, you can easily find it on YouTube or iTunes by searching "the trumpet shall sound.") The text used in this music is 1 Corinthians 15:52, 53. First read the verses aloud in your Bible, then listen to the music and consider how it illustrates Paul's words in this passage.

Handel is famous for using "word painting"—the idea that the music, just like paint on canvas, illustrates for us what is happening in the text. There are several good examples of word painting in this portion of *Messiah*. Listen to the piece a few times to notice some of the word painting in this piece (doing so will also help you memorize the text). As you listen (and perhaps sing along), invite God to speak to you through the words and the music.

You may want to use the following questions to help you discover the word painting:

- How does the music illustrate the phrase, "The dead shall be raised"?
- Listen to the end of the piece. What happens? How is the music written to demonstrate how "we shall be changed"?
- What other parts of this piece demonstrate the glory of the resurrection?

Study written by Joy-Elizabeth Lawrence. She is a writer, actor, and staff member of Calvin College. In her graduate work, her studies focused on the theology of the body and the resurrection.

WHAT IS THE KINGDOM OF GOD?

{ UNDERSTANDING HOW NEAR THE KINGDOM OF HEAVEN REALLY IS }

PREPARE

Before you meet with your small group, read this good question. Then read the response article written by Christopher A. Hall.

GQ 6 **What is the difference between the heavenly "paradise" that Christ promised the thief on the cross and the kingdom of God?**

In all likelihood, we should make a distinction between the paradise Jesus promised the thief on the cross and the kingdom of God.

How so? From the inception of Jesus' ministry, he announced the arrival of the kingdom of God in his teaching and his actions. In Mark 1:15, shortly after Jesus' baptism and temptation in the wilderness, he preaches that "the kingdom of God is near. Repent and believe the gospel." In Matthew 12 Jesus clearly states that "if I drive out demons by the Spirit of God, then the kingdom of God has come upon you."

An unexpected overlap between the ages thus occurs. Sickness, demon possession, injustice, and death characterize this present evil age. *Through his healing, exorcisms, concern for the poor and oppressed, and raising people from the dead, Jesus indicates the arrival of the kingdom age. Through Christ, God's kingdom—the life of the age to come—is breaking into the midst of this present evil age.*

The dying thief on the cross grasped that which Jesus' disciples had difficulty understanding. At Caesarea Philippi Jesus began to teach that he must go up to Jerusalem, suffer, be rejected by the elders and teachers of the law, be killed, and after three days rise from the dead (Mark 8:31). This message of a suffering, crucified Messiah made little sense to Jesus' contemporaries. Neither Jesus' closest disciples nor his enemies could comprehend how the anointed of God could also be the cursed of God. A crucified Messiah seemed to be a contradiction in terms.

The crucified thief, though, possessed an insight that almost everyone else at Jesus' execution lacked. The believing thief asks Jesus to remember him when he comes into his kingdom (Luke 23:42). As Maximus of Turin rightly preached, "The penitent thief considered the cross of Christ not to be a stumbling block."

Jesus promised the thief that "today you will be with me in paradise." Paradise, then, seems to be a specific place or state of being. This is distinct from the kingdom of God—a broader reality referring to an age of God's reign as well as the place of its full manifestation.

Interestingly, immediate entrance into paradise is linked to faith in the coming of Christ's kingdom. As Leon Morris puts it, "Jesus' words of reassurance gave [the thief] more than he had asked for. Not only would he have a place in the kingdom, whenever that would be established, but that very day he would enter Paradise."

Both modern scholars and the church fathers link paradise with the Garden of Eden. In his commentary The Gospel of Luke, I. Howard Marshall, for instance, notes that the connection between Eden and paradise led "to the view that [paradise] existed in between the creation and the final age in hidden form. It came to be regarded as the intermediate resting place for the souls of the righteous dead. . . . In the present passage it represents the state of bliss which Jesus promises to the criminal directly after death."

> Through Christ, God's kingdom—the life of the age to come—is breaking into the midst of this present evil age.

Not only does Christ's priestly work on the cross enable him as king to open the doors of paradise to the thief, but it also reverses the horror of what took place in the Garden of Eden. St. John Chrysostom observes that when Christ "wished to bring the thief into paradise, he immediately spoke the word and brought him in. Christ did not need to pray to do this . . . . God put there the flaming sword to guard paradise (Genesis 3:24). By his authority Christ opened paradise and brought in the thief."

Entrance into paradise is available not only to the thief but to all who put their trust in Christ. Origen comments that Christ "gave to all those who believe and confess access to the entrance that Adam had previously closed by sinning. Who else could remove 'the flaming turning sword which was placed to guard the tree of life' and the gates of paradise?" To enter paradise is to return, in Prudentius' poignant phrase, to "our native country."

Christ will return one day with all the inhabitants of paradise to consummate his reign on earth. In the meantime, those who die confessing (with the believing thief) faith in Christ's kingdom can rest assured they will be with Christ in paradise during the strange, unexpected in-between time between Jesus' first and second coming.

Christopher A. Hall is Chancellor of Eastern University in St. Davids, Pennsylvania, and a Christianity Today editor-at-large. "Christ's Kingdom and Paradise" was first published in the November 2003 issue of Christianity Today.

LAUNCH

OPTIONAL EXERCISE

Your group may want to begin your meeting with this activity. You'll need **paper** and **pens**.

Begin thinking together about what it means to be a citizen by creating two fictional countries. Break into two equal-sized groups; each group should spend five to ten minutes devising the identity of your new, made-up country. (Your efforts can be serious, wacky, or anything in between.) Each country group should select and complete three of the activities below:

- Pick a country name.
- Write a short Bill of Rights for your country (no more than ten points). For example, free speech, freedom of religion, the right to vote, and so on.
- Draw a flag.
- Write a national anthem and sing it for the other group.
- Define citizenship within your country and who can be a citizen.

Get back together to present your countries to each other, then talk through some of these questions:

• Are you proud of your country's name, flag, or anthem?
• How did you decide what would be in your Bill of Rights?
• How did you decide who could be a citizen?
• Did your country represent you as a person and as a follower of Jesus? Why or why not?

Many of us have been asked, "If you were to die today, do you know where you would go?" Perhaps we've also asked this question of others in an effort to share our faith. It's often used to prompt people to think about the important issue of life after death.

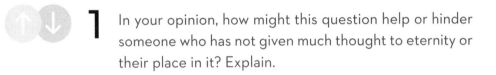

1 In your opinion, how might this question help or hinder someone who has not given much thought to eternity or their place in it? Explain.

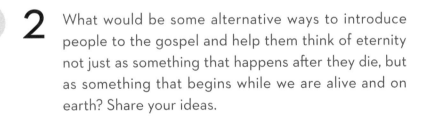

2 What would be some alternative ways to introduce people to the gospel and help them think of eternity not just as something that happens after they die, but as something that begins while we are alive and on earth? Share your ideas.

The kingdom of God is a present reality, but it can often be overlooked when we're talking to someone about salvation and eternity. Yet the Bible is clear: there is a critical connection between the way we think about Heaven (future) and how we understand our citizenship in the kingdom of God (now).

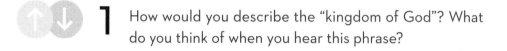

ENGAGE

THE KINGDOM OF GOD IS AT HAND!

The kingdom of God was one of Jesus' most frequent teaching themes. Many of his original followers misunderstood his teachings on the kingdom, and even for us today the kingdom can be hard to comprehend.

1 How would you describe the "kingdom of God"? What do you think of when you hear this phrase?

As a group, read **Psalm 103:15-19; 145:8-13; Mark 1:14, 15; 10:13-16;** and **Luke 17:20, 21.**

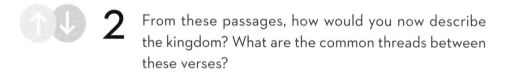

2 From these passages, how would you now describe the kingdom? What are the common threads between these verses?

The ministry of Jesus ushered in the kingdom of God. As Christopher Hall notes, "Through his healing, exorcisms, concern for the poor and oppressed, and raising people from the dead, Jesus indicates the arrival of the kingdom age." Essentially, the kingdom of

God is his reign over all the earth. The whole world belongs to him and one day it will recognize God as sovereign over all.

Jesus' radical teachings about the new covenant, grace, mercy, servanthood, justice, and God's love are all facets of his kingdom. These values of the kingdom are exemplified in Jesus' ministry and are in direct opposition to the ways of the world. God's reign, however, will only be fully realized when Jesus returns and reigns on the renewed earth (see Revelation 21). In this sense, the kingdom of God is *both* a present and future reality; it is already here, but it is not yet fully realized.[1]

DELVE DEEPER

If you'd like, explore this question as a group or on your own:

Jesus tells a series of parables in Matthew 13 to describe the kingdom of Heaven. The phrase "the kingdom of the heavens" is unique to Matthew "where heavens is a substitute for the divine name." The "kingdom of heaven" has the same meaning as the "kingdom of God"—Matthew just says it differently to appeal to his Jewish audience.[2]

Read Matthew 13; as you do, create a list describing what the kingdom of Heaven is like based on this passage.

Which of these parables did you most resonate with? Why? Why do you think Jesus used stories like this to teach about the kingdom?

The kingdom of God is different from Heaven (or "paradise"). When we die, we will be in Heaven. But until that happens, we are to live to give witness to God's kingdom. Unfortunately, followers of Jesus are often far more concerned with the heavenly afterlife than with our role as ambassadors of the kingdom during our lives here on earth.

3 Why do you think Christians often put greater focus and emphasis on Heaven (paradise) than on the kingdom of God? (Take into consideration songs we sing, ways we evangelize, and popular books.)

WE ARE CITIZENS OF THE KINGDOM OF GOD

Citizenship in a particular country can carry a lot of weight. For anyone traveling abroad, one's own citizenship can be a badge of honor or, conversely, an invitation for trouble. In Philippians 3:20, Paul writes to believers that "our citizenship is in heaven. And we eagerly await a Savior from there, the Lord Jesus Christ."

 4 What does it mean to be a citizen of your country? (If you have ever traveled abroad, share what it felt like to be an alien in another country.)

 5 What are the differences between your citizenship in Heaven and in your home country?

Read **1 Peter 2:9-12** out loud as a group. In this passage, Peter borrows language that God used for Israel at Mt. Sinai in Exodus 19:5, 6 and reapplies it to the church. While Israel for a time was considered a theocracy (a country governed by priests in the name of God), Peter's audience was the church living under Roman rule.

6 What did it mean for Israel to be a "holy nation" (in Exodus)? What did it mean for the church living in the first century? What do you think it means for us today? Explain.

We will inevitably experience tension as we live, in a sense, in two worlds. "Christians understand themselves as citizens of two kingdoms," theologian Marva Dawn writes, "[W]e live in our wealthy society and also in the kingdom of God, our parallel culture . . . [where] we proclaim in worship the truth—until we know that truth so well that we can say to the surrounding culture, 'We don't believe your lies anymore,' and that opens up a trembling freedom to change it!"[3] As kingdom citizens, we're to live by the values of God's heavenly kingdom. We're called to be a moral witness to our society in both our words and deeds.

> ### DELVE DEEPER
> If you'd like, explore this question as a group or on your own:
>
> Following Peter's section on the church being a "holy nation," he urges his audience to submit to the governing authorities (kings, presidents) and to submit to those who rule. Read 1 Peter 2:13-21.
>
> How can you both live as a citizen of a holy nation and submit to ruling authorities? Do you feel disobedience to the ruling authorities is ever allowed? If so, when?

7 Romans 12:1-13:7 outlines our lives as dual citizens. Read the passage, then discuss Paul's call to the church and his instructions for living as a citizen of an earthly country. What do you think Paul's main point is in this passage? Summarize it in your own words on the next page.

JESUS CHRIST COMMISSIONS US TO INVITE OTHERS INTO THE KINGDOM

Read **Matthew 28:16-20**. Here, Jesus asserted his authority and commanded his disciples to go and make more disciples. The Great Commission was not the first time he had told his disciples to go. Luke 9:1-6 succinctly describes the first time Jesus sent them to drive out demons, heal the sick, and preach the kingdom of God.

 8 Read **Luke 9:1-6.** How do you think the disciples' first experience of being sent by Jesus informed how they understood the Great Commission (in Matthew 28:16-20)? What do you see as the major similarities and differences between these two events?

Jesus spent time with his followers for forty days after his resurrection specifically speaking about the kingdom of God (Acts 1:3-8). When it was time for Jesus to ascend to Heaven, he said they would be his witnesses in Jerusalem, Judea, and Samaria and to the ends of the earth.

9 Read **Acts 1:1-11.** How do Jesus' parting words in Acts 1:7, 8 compare or contrast with the Great Commission (Matthew 28:16-20)? Why do you think the Holy Spirit and "authority" are mentioned in each passage?

Becoming a citizen of the kingdom of God isn't like the ultimate country club membership, guaranteeing a cushy heavenly abode! Those who truly understand Jesus' profound grace and forgiveness know better than to hang around by the pool or play golf waiting for their eternal inheritance. They instead live out the teachings of Jesus and embody his example of loving sacrifice for fellow believers and the world. As Jonathan R. Wilson wrote in his book *Why Church Matters,* "The work that Jesus calls us to is to bear witness to the kingdom of God and call people to life in that kingdom (life in Christ) by our words and our deeds. . . . Jesus' words and his deeds proclaim the kingdom of God; so should ours."[4]

10 In light of all you've discussed, how do you feel inspired to bear witness to the kingdom of God in your everyday life? Share a specific idea.

RESPOND

In your group, imagine together an evangelism conversation with a spiritually curious friend. How might you explain the gospel message to your friend in light of this discussion about the kingdom of God? Explain.

REACT

Living out the values of the kingdom of God can be summarized in two major categories: becoming more like Jesus Christ and making disciples. In the space below, write your thoughts about how you are doing in each category. Is one area stronger than the other or are they about the same? In general, how can you better live out kingdom values through the power of the Holy Spirit?

Pray as a group about kingdom living—both becoming more like Jesus Christ and making disciples. Pray also that we could take seriously the authority by which we are sent, the power of the Holy Spirit, and the grace and forgiveness we have received.

STRETCH

Set aside time on your own after your small group meeting to build relationships with non-Christians.

In order to live out kingdom values and "go and make disciples," we actually need to rub shoulders with those who do not know Jesus Christ personally. This week, set aside time to meet new people and to reach out to those you already know.

If you are not currently involved in an externally-focused ministry in your church, then do some research and find out how you can get involved. There is no need to reinvent the wheel if there is already a natural way to connect and serve your neighborhood through your church. You can also invite your small group to participate.

Think about the daily, weekly, and monthly rhythm of your life. Are there already people you naturally come in contact with who do not know Jesus? How can you be more kingdom-minded in your interactions with them? If you can't think of anyone, then maybe you need to make some changes to get out of the "Christian bubble" a bit.

Share your thoughts and ideas with your small group or a friend . . . then "go and make disciples"!

FOR FURTHER STUDY
BOOKS

- *Becoming a Contagious Christian* by Bill Hybels and Mark Mittelberg (Zondervan)
- *Beyond Your Backyard* by Tom Ellsworth (Standard Publishing)
- *The Gospel in a Pluralist Society* by Lesslie Newbigin (Eerdmans)
- *The Master Plan of Evangelism* by Robert E. Coleman (Revell)
- *The Scandal of the Evangelical Conscience* by Ronald J. Sider (Baker Books)
- *The Teaching of Jesus Concerning the Kingdom of God and the Church* by Geerhardus Vos (Nabu Press)
- *Unfettered Hope: A Call to Faithful Living in an Affluent Society* by Marva J. Dawn (Westminster John Knox Press)

ONLINE ARTICLES

- "The Changing Face of Apologetics," interview of Lee Strobel by Stan Guthrie, from *Christianity Today* (www.christianitytoday.com/ct/2009/june/22.58.html)
- "Come, Lord Jesus" by Carolyn Arends, from *Christianity Today* (www.christianitytoday.com/ct/2009/october/22.60.html)
- "Kingdom-Driven Church" by John Nugent, from *Christian Standard* (christianstandard.com/2005/09/cs-article-106/)

Study written by Jason and Alison Tarka.
Jason and Alison live in Portland, Oregon, where Jason leads worship, teaches theology, and writes for small groups. Alison is a stay-at-home mother, violinist, blogger, and freelance writer.

• NOTES •

SESSION 1

1. John Swinton and Richard Payne, eds., *Living Well and Dying Faithfully: Christian Practices for End-of-Life Care* (Grand Rapids: Eerdmans, 2009), xii–xiii.

2. N. T. Wright, *Surprised by Hope*, (New York: HarperOne, 2008), 179.

SESSION 2

1. C. Stephen Evans, *Philosophy of Religion* (Downers Grove: Inter-Varsity Press, 1982), 175.

2. Craig L. Blomberg, *The New American Commentary: Matthew* (Nashville: Broadman Press, 1992), 142.

3. Gordon R. Lewis and Bruce A. Demarest, *Integrative Theology* (Grand Rapids: Zondervan, 1996), 184–197.

4. Evans, *Philosophy of Religion,* 179.

5. Information in this section was taken from the following sources: "Eternal Destinations: Americans Believe in Heaven, Hell," Gallup, http://www.gallup.com/poll/11770/eternal-destinations -americans-believe-heaven-hell.aspx (accessed November 9, 2010); Michael Paulson, "What Lies Beneath," *Boston Globe,* June 29, 2008, http://www.boston.com/bostonglobe/ideas/articles/2008/06/29/ what_lies_beneath/, accessed November 9, 2010; and "Americans Describe Their Views About Life After Death," Barna Group, www .barna.org/barna-update/article/5-barna-update/128-americans

-describe-their-views-about-life-after-death?q=hell (accessed November 9, 2010).

SESSION 3

1. James I. Packer, "Evangelical Annihilationism in Review," *Reformation & Revival,* Spring 1997; (also at www.the-highway.com/annihilationism_Packer.html, accessed November 9, 2010).

2. David L. Edwards and John Stott, *Evangelical Essentials*, (Downers Grove: InterVarsity, 1989), 315–316.

3. Leonard Sweet, Brian D. McLaren, and Jerry Haselmayer, *A is for Abductive* (Grand Rapids: Zondervan, 2003), 186.

SESSION 4

1. Erwin W. Lutzer, *One Minute After You Die* (Chicago: Moody Press, 1997), 83.

2. Frederich Nietzsche, http://thequotationspage.com (accessed August 3, 2010); also Frederich Nietzsche, *The Will to Power,* Walter Kaufmann and R. J. Hollingdale, trans., (New York: Vintage Books, 1967), 467.

3. Randy Alcorn, *Heaven* (Wheaton, Illinois: Tyndale House Publishers, 2004), 166.

4. Sean McDowell, "What Will Heaven Be Like?" Worldview Ministries, www.seanmcdowell.org/media/articles/theology/heaven.asp (accessed August 3, 2010).

5. Warren Wiersbe, *The Bible Exposition Commentary: New Testament Volume 2* in the WordSearch library (WordSearch Corporation, 2005).

SESSION 5

1. D. J. A. Clines, "The Image of God in Man," *Tyndale Bulletin* 19 (1968): 53–103.

2. Joy-Elizabeth Lawrence, *Flesh That Needs to be Loved: A Christian Dialogue with Toni Morrison's* Beloved *and* Paradise (Thesis, Regent College, 2005).

3. Craig A. Evans and Stanley E. Porter, eds., *IVP Dictionary of New Testament Background* (Downers Grove: InterVarsity Press, 2000), 416.

SESSION 6

1. The idea of the kingdom of God being "already" but "not yet" was first coined by theologian Geerhurdus Vos in his work *The Teaching of Jesus Concerning the Kingdom of God and the Church.*

2. George Eldon Ladd, *A Theology of the New Testament* (Grand Rapids: Eerdmans, 2002), 61.

3. Marva J. Dawn; *Unfettered Hope: A Call to Faithful Living in an Affluent Society* (Louisville: Westminster John Knox Press, 2003), 195–196.

4. Jonathan R. Wilson, *Why Church Matters: Worship, Ministry, and Mission in Practice* (Grand Rapids: Brazos Press, 2006), 83.

GOOD QUESTION BIBLE STUDIES SERIES CONTRIBUTORS

• ARTICLE AUTHORS •

D. A. Carson is research professor of New Testament at Trinity Evangelical Divinity School.

Timothy George is dean of Beeson Divinity School of Samford University and an executive editor of *Christianity Today*.

Stanley J. Grenz was professor of theology at Carey/Regent College in Vancouver, British Columbia, Canada, and at Northern Baptist Theological Seminary in Illinois.

Christopher A. Hall is professor of biblical and theological studies at Eastern University in St. Davids, Pennsylvania, and a *Christianity Today* editor-at-large.

Craig S. Keener is a visiting professor at Eastern Seminary in Philadelphia and author of *The IVP Bible Background Commentary: New Testament*.

R. Todd Mangum is Professor of Theology and Dean of the Faculty at Biblical Seminary in Hatfield, Pennsylvania.

Alister McGrath is Professor of Theology, Ministry and Education, and Head of the Center for Theology, Religion, and Culture at King's College, London. He is the author of many books, including *Mere Theology* and *The Dawkins Delusion?*

Roger E. Olson is professor of theology at George W. Truett Theological Seminary of Baylor University and author of *The Westminster Handbook to Evangelical Theology*.

Nancy Ortberg is a church leadership consultant and popular speaker. Formerly a teaching pastor at Willow Creek Community Church in Illinois, she now lives in California with her husband, John.

J. I. Packer is Board of Governors' Professor of Theology at Regent College and a member of the editorial council for *Christianity Today*.

Arthur O. Roberts is professor-at-large at George Fox University and author of *Exploring Heaven: What Great Christian Thinkers Tell Us About Our Afterlife with God* (HarperSanFrancisco).

Bruce Shelley was church history professor at Denver Seminary.

Lewis B. Smedes was professor emeritus of theology and ethics at Fuller Theological Seminary and author of *The Art of Forgiving: When You Need to Forgive and Don't Know How*.

Allen Verhey is a professor of Christian Ethics at Duke Divinity School.

• BIBLE STUDY AUTHORS •

Tracey Bianchi is the Pastor for Women at Christ Church of Oak Brook and is an activist, writer, and speaker on Christians and the environment. She earned her MDiv from Denver Seminary. You can visit her at traceybianchi.com.

Christopher Blumhofer is an ordination candidate in the Presbyterian church. His writings have appeared in *Leadership* journal, *Relevant*, and BuildingChurchLeaders.com.

Amie Hollman is a freelance writer, graphic designer, and illustrator who has contributed work for *Radiant, Sojourners, Neue* online, *Light & Life*, and the *LIVE Bible* (NLT). She lives with her family in New York City, where her husband is a pastor at a multicultural church in Queens.

Jan Johnson is the author of twenty books, including *Invitation to the Jesus Life*, and many magazine articles and Bible studies. Also a speaker and spiritual director, she holds a DMin in Ignatian spirituality (www.JanJohnson.org).

Joy-Elizabeth Lawrence is a writer, actor, coauthor of *Grand Days*, and a staff member at Calvin College. You can find her at www.joyelizabethlawrence.wordpress.com.

Michael Mack is the Life Groups Minister at Northeast Christian Church in Louisville, Kentucky. He is founder of SmallGroups.com and SmallGroupLeadership.com, and has written numerous books about small group leadership, including *I'm a Leader . . . Now What?* (Standard Publishing).

Kevin Miller served for many years as Vice President at Christianity Today International. He recently left CTI to pursue full-time ministry as a pastor in the Chicago area.

Jason and Alison Tarka are writers and musicians. They pastor and minister together in an urban church in Portland, Oregon.

David Trujillo is a Bible teacher, adult ministry leader, and a columnist for *GROUP* magazine.

Kelli B. Trujillo is an adult ministry leader and the author of several books, including *Faith-Filled Moments* (Wesleyan).

Kyle White is the founding director of Neighbors' House, an outreach to at-risk students in DeKalb County, Illinois. He is a freelance writer, frequent contributor to Christian BibleStudies.com, and author of *Wisconsin River of Grace*. Kyle can be found at KyleLWhite.blogspot.com.

Heather Gemmen Wilson is a best-selling author and an award-winning international speaker. She is married to a pastor, and together they have six children.

ADDITIONAL BOOKS IN THE GOOD QUESTION SERIES

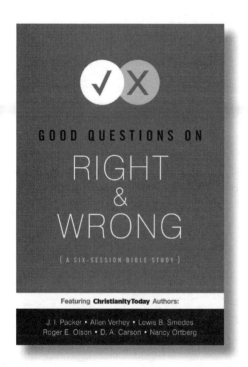

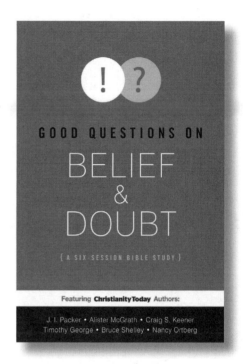

Good Questions on Right & Wrong

Considering these questions:
- Can lying ever be justified?
- Are all sins equal?
- Should Christians take care of the earth?

Item # 021556610

Good Questions on Belief & Doubt

Considering these questions:
- Why does God answer some prayers for healing but not mine?
- If Jesus was God, how could the eternal God die?
- How do I determine which Scriptures apply today?

Item #021556710